I0814287

INDUSTRY JOBS

JOBS IN TRANSPORTATION

BY KAREN MASERJIAN SHAN

Core Library

An Imprint of Abdo Publishing
abdobooks.com

Cover image: Ground crew workers help service planes, clear runways, and do maintenance work at airports.

abdobooks.com

Published by Abdo Publishing, a division of ABDO, PO Box 398166, Minneapolis, Minnesota 55439.

Printed in the United States of America, North Mankato, Minnesota.
052023
092023

Cover Photo: Shutterstock Images
Interior Photos: Marcel Kusch/DPA Picture Alliance/Alamy, 4–5; Robert Alexander/Archive Photos/Getty Images, 8; Red Line Editorial, 10, 31; Shutterstock Images, 12–13; Jeffrey Greenberg/UCG/Universal Images Group/Getty Images, 15; Khaled Desouki/AFP/Getty Images, 17, 42 (bottom); Boris Roessler/DPA/Picture Alliance/Getty Images, 18–19; Tech. Sgt. Drew A. Egnoske/US Air National Guard/US Air Force, 21; Axel Heimken/DPA/Picture Alliance/Getty Images, 23, 42 (middle bottom); Robert Nickelsberg/Getty Images News/Getty Images, 24, 43 (bottom); Muhammed Enes Yildirim/Anadolu Agency/Getty Images, 26–27, 43 (middle top); Kardasov Films/Shutterstock Images, 29; iStockphoto, 34–35, 36, 42 (middle top), 43 (middle); NamLong Nguyen/Shutterstock Images, 39; Xavier Arnau/iStockphoto, 42 (top); Yasuyoshi Chiba/AFP/Getty Images, 42 (middle); Kali9/E+/Getty Images, 43 (top), 45; Sinology/Moment/Getty Images, 43 (middle bottom)

Editor: Laura Stickney
Series Designer: Katharine Hale

Library of Congress Control Number: 2022949099

Publisher's Cataloging-in-Publication Data
Names: Maserjian Shan, Karen, author.
Title: Jobs in transportation / by Karen Maserjian Shan
Description: Minneapolis, Minnesota: Abdo Publishing Company, 2024 | Series: Industry jobs | Includes online resources and index.
Identifiers: ISBN 9781098290900 (lib. bdg.) | ISBN 9781098277086 (ebook)
Subjects: LCSH: Occupations--Juvenile literature. | Transportation--Biography--Juvenile literature. | Transportation industry--Biography--Juvenile literature.
Classification: DDC 380.5--dc23

CONTENTS

CHAPTER ONE

LIFE AS A RAIL TRAFFIC CONTROLLER

Steven turns from the computer monitors on his desk and answers the phone. He works at the city's railroad control center. As a rail traffic controller, Steven often receives calls by phone and radio. The calls are from people who drive passenger trains and freight trains. They report on the conditions of the city's trains and track lines. Like the other rail traffic controllers in his department, Steven works to make sure the city's trains move to and from their destinations safely and on time.

Rail traffic controllers must understand how a railroad operates. They must plan carefully to reduce traffic delays along the tracks.

TRAFFIC MANAGEMENT

Drivers and pilots are among the most visible workers in transporting people and goods. Behind the scenes, transportation supervisors and coordinators keep things running smoothly. They direct and manage tasks. They also oversee how vehicles are used and where they're driven. They plan schedules for drivers, too. Schedules help drivers know where they need to drive and when they need to pick up or deliver cargo. Supervisors also manage the budgets for transportation equipment. They help keep vehicles in good shape.

The phone call is from an engineer. He says a tree has fallen across a train track. The train is stopped. Steven moves into action, alerting separate railroad crews. He tells the workers who control the tracks' electricity to turn the power off. He also speaks with a team that can move the fallen tree from the tracks. Then he tells the crew that maintains the tracks to fix any damage the tree might have caused. Steven also contacts the bus center. He asks them to have buses pick up the passengers from the stopped train and take them where they need to go.

Steven loves being at the heart of the city's train lines. He knows people and businesses rely on him and his team to help them travel safely. He likes having new challenges to tackle every day.

FROM HERE TO THERE

Imagine going to a grocery store only to find its shelves empty or going to a pharmacy that doesn't have any medicine. Pantries and shelves in homes, stores, medical centers, and businesses need to be stocked with supplies. People working in transportation help make this possible. They drive, pilot, and maintain delivery vehicles. They bring supplies to places in need, keeping shelves full. From trains and trucks to ships and airplanes, each mode of transportation brings the world together in important ways.

In the United States, more than 8 million people work in transportation jobs. These workers have a

Some delivery drivers work for large companies like the United Parcel Service (UPS). They deliver packages to homes and businesses.

variety of jobs. Some drive ground vehicles or pilot aircraft. Others help stranded passenger vehicles. Some people manage traffic patterns, transportation teams, or equipment. Specialists coordinate how passengers and products are transported to their destinations.

Transportation workers also help maintain equipment and keep vehicles moving. They make sure all the actions needed to move people and products are performed smoothly and safely.

Most jobs in transportation involve teamwork. Every day and night of the year, transportation teams are hard at work. They make sure people and products get to their destinations on time and in good condition.

PERSPECTIVES

THE FUTURE OF TRANSPORTATION

The skills needed for jobs in transportation will change over time. This is because of new technologies that are making vehicles and travel safer. Some of these changes include the way vehicles are powered. For example, electric vehicles run on electricity instead of gasoline. Working with electric vehicles requires new skills. Jesus Rojas works at an auto repair shop. He said, "I'm not against electric vehicles. I've always loved cars and I'll work on them until I can't anymore. So we have to adjust. We have to get out of our comfort zones."

PAY FOR TRANSPORTATION WORKERS

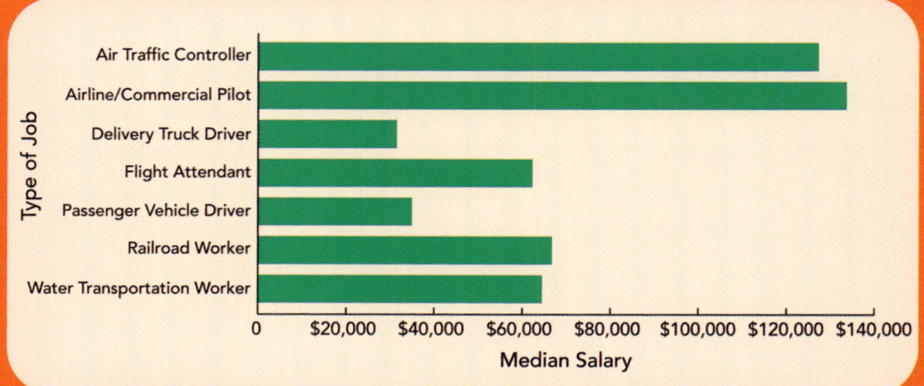

In 2021, air traffic controllers and airline pilots earned the highest median salaries out of the transportation jobs shown above. A median salary is the middle point of salaries within a field. Air traffic controllers and pilots also require the most training. Why do you think people with these jobs earn higher salaries?

TRAINING AND EDUCATION

Different transportation careers require specific types of schooling, training, and experience. Most positions require a high school diploma or college degree. On-the-job training or additional coursework may also be needed. For some jobs, workers must earn a special license or certification. Other positions require training through special programs, online institutions, or trade schools that train people for specific jobs.

Certain personal qualities can also be useful, such as friendliness and good organizational skills. Transportation workers must work well in teams and know how to manage their time effectively. These skills are important for people working with transportation on the ground, in the air, and on the water.

FURTHER EVIDENCE

Chapter One discusses teamwork in transportation jobs. Identify one of the chapter's main points. Listen to transportation engineer Yung Koprowski at the website below. Find a quote from the video that supports the author's main point.

ON THE MOVE

abdocorelibrary.com/jobs-in-transportation

CHAPTER TWO

ON THE GROUND

Many transportation workers operate vehicles that travel on roads and train tracks. These vehicles go over land, across bridges, and through tunnels. Workers load, drive, and unpack trucks and trains to deliver supplies. They also transport people.

Truck drivers spend long periods of time on roadways. They may drive small delivery trucks or large trucks. Many truck drivers transport packages and equipment to places near and far away. This takes strength

Long-haul truck drivers travel long distances, often covering more than 250 miles (402 km). They must be prepared for all kinds of road conditions.

and energy. Drivers must be prepared to load heavy cargo and drive long distances.

SAFE DRIVING

Truck and bus drivers must follow safe driving practices to protect passengers and people nearby. Drivers should check their vehicles' mirrors for other vehicles. Because their vehicles are so large, truck drivers should make sure they have enough room to turn and stop their vehicles. They must wear seat belts and follow the speed limit. It's also important for truck drivers to be well rested. They need to stay alert while driving, especially when traveling long distances. Drivers should keep their vehicles properly maintained and pay attention to road and weather conditions.

Some truck drivers buy or rent trucks. They operate their own trucking businesses. These drivers are called owner-operators. They run their businesses by finding companies that need cargo delivered. They also plan schedules to keep their businesses running smoothly.

Truck drivers usually need a high school diploma. They must have a driver's license and a

Bus drivers are responsible for assisting passengers as they board the bus. They may operate equipment such as wheelchair lifts.

good driving record. Long-haul truck drivers also need a commercial driver's license, or CDL. To get a CDL, drivers must pass special tests.

BUS DRIVERS

Bus drivers transport people to various places. Drivers can work day or night because people always need to travel. Bus drivers can work part-time or full-time for up to 40 hours a week.

These drivers operate different kinds of buses. School bus drivers take students to and from school. Intercity bus drivers transport people on scheduled routes. They collect fare money and tickets

PERSPECTIVES
WORKING HOURS

Transportation drivers sometimes work long shifts, which can be tiring. It also means workers have less time to spend with their families. Jeff Kurtz was a railroad employee for 40 years. He said tiredness from long workdays is a problem for many railroad workers. It can be extra uncomfortable for workers who spend their days in the train's cab. This small space is where the controls are located. Kurtz was once on a train traveling through an ice storm. Even though his planned work day was over, he had to stay on the train for more than 20 additional hours. "You don't recover from that for a long time," he said.

from passengers. They also answer questions about bus schedules and routes. These drivers travel on city streets, stopping to pick up and drop off passengers.

Most bus drivers have a high school diploma and receive on-the-job training. All positions require a driver's license.

RAILWAY WORKERS

Locomotive engineers drive trains that carry people and cargo.

Locomotive engineers pay close attention to their surroundings while driving trains. They must know how to operate many different controls and watch for obstacles on the track.

They use controls to operate the locomotive. They also oversee a train's speed.

Other railway workers keep passengers safe. Conductors check tickets, announce travel information, and make sure passengers are comfortable. On freight trains, conductors also manage how cargo is loaded.

Some workers keep train equipment in good condition. They adjust brakes, signals, and switches. Other people work within the rail yard, which is a set of tracks where trains are sorted, loaded, and unloaded. Rail yard engineers operate train engines at rail yards, while yardmasters handle worker activity.

LUFTRETTUNG

CHAPTER THREE

IN THE AIR

Airplanes and other aircraft also play a role in transporting people and goods. Workers fly, direct, and maintain airplanes, helicopters, and other flying machines. They work with aircraft used for business and vacation travel, military flights, medical needs, and even agriculture.

Some of the most important transportation workers are pilots. They fly and navigate airplanes, helicopters, and other aircraft. They transport people, equipment, and supplies to

Some pilots fly emergency medical service helicopters. They help transport patients to hospitals quickly and safely.

FLYING FOR THE MILITARY

Military pilots fly military aircraft for hundreds of missions. These aircraft are used to transport goods and people, view specific areas from above, investigate events, and train people. Aircraft are used for combat missions, too. In the United States, military pilots work for the Army, Air Force, Navy, or National Guard. To become military pilots, people complete a four-year college degree. Then they enter the military and complete pilot training.

distant places. When flying, military pilots must closely observe what is happening around them in the air and on the ground. They use their aircraft's controls and systems to fly the aircraft. They watch monitors that show weather conditions. Pilots also communicate with air traffic controllers to adjust the aircraft's flight path.

Airline pilots fly aircraft for airlines. They transport people and cargo according to a set schedule. These aircraft are staffed by two pilots, the captain and copilot. The captain is responsible for the flight, its crew,

Pilots must know how to operate aircraft controls, monitor fuel usage, and adapt to changing weather conditions while in the air.

and its passengers or cargo. The copilot works with the captain. These aviators need a college degree. They may also need to complete flight training with qualified flight instructors. Some schools have flight training programs for people who wish to become pilots.

PERSPECTIVES

PROMOTING FEMALE PILOTS

Many women work as pilots for airlines and the military. But in the early 1900s, many men thought women were not strong or smart enough to be pilots. In 2020, female airline pilots represented just over 5 percent of all commercial airline pilots worldwide. Part of the problem is a lack of role models. Pamela Perdue is a captain with United Airlines. She says that when passengers see her, they often say they've never seen a female pilot. "It starts a dialogue that allows me to promote the profession, specifically as it pertains to young women," she says.

Pilots need a range of skills in the fields of math, physics, and technology.

AIR TRAFFIC CONTROLLERS

Air traffic controllers manage aircraft movement. They guide pilots and monitor weather conditions. They use radar and computers to direct pilots flying aircraft. They communicate with pilots to help them steer their aircraft in the sky and on the ground. This helps prevent aircraft collisions. Air traffic controllers often manage multiple

Air traffic controllers must be able to communicate effectively and make quick decisions. This keeps aircraft safe and on schedule.

aircraft at the same time. For instance, they may direct the landing of one aircraft while providing a weather update to another aircraft.

Air traffic controllers need several years of experience working with aircraft. Most positions require a bachelor's degree or associate degree in a field such as transportation, aviation, or engineering. Most people also need special training from a qualified air traffic program. They must also pass medical exams, tests, and training courses.

Flight attendants help make flights more comfortable for passengers. They serve snacks and beverages, demonstrate how to use safety gear, and answer questions during flights.

FLIGHT ATTENDANTS

Flight attendants take care of airline passengers and handle onboard emergencies. They help passengers find their seats and store their bags. They show passengers how to use an oxygen mask and other emergency equipment. On some flights, they provide snacks.

Most flight attendant positions require a high school diploma. Some airlines prefer flight attendants to have college degrees, too. Flight attendants also undergo special training. They must be certified by the Federal Aviation Administration (FAA). Flight attendants who fly internationally may need to know other languages.

EXPLORE ONLINE

Chapter Three discusses the training needed to become a pilot. The website below explains more about how to become a pilot. Does the website answer any of the questions you had about working as a pilot? What new information did you learn from the website?

HOW TO BECOME AN AIRLINE OR COMMERCIAL PILOT

abdocorelibrary.com/jobs-in-transportation

CHAPTER FOUR

ON THE WATER

Some transportation jobs involve working on rivers, lakes, and oceans. People work on ships and boats that transport equipment, supplies, and passengers over waterways. They use a variety of watercraft, including ferries, cruise ships, cargo ships, and US Navy ships. These transportation workers direct their watercraft from home-based ports to distant ports. Sometimes they travel across oceans to ports on foreign coasts.

Ship captains can work on many different kinds of ships, including ferries, fishing boats, and tugboats.

WORKING AS A SHIP CAPTAIN

Ship captains spend most of their time working outdoors in all kinds of weather. They must wear protective clothing such as gloves and rain gear. They must be prepared to work in bright outdoor light or very dim light. Captains also work with heavy equipment and dangerous materials. The difficult conditions mean that ship captains must make quick decisions, be good problem-solvers, and perform tasks accurately in order to keep their crews safe.

Ships and boats are commanded by captains or masters, who steer and operate the vessels. These workers also direct a watercraft's crew and coordinate how the boat moves through the water. Ship captains are responsible for ordering equipment for their ships and overseeing passengers as they board and disembark. Captains need to know how to steer their watercraft and obey all safety laws.

Ship engineers maintain important equipment on a ship. They do repairs, keep the engine room running, and make sure machinery works properly.

PERSPECTIVES

NEW TECHNOLOGIES

New technologies are changing how water vessels are built and operated. Dr. Cleopatra Doumbia-Henry is president of the World Maritime University. In 2020, she spoke on how new technologies have changed maritime transportation and how they will continue to have an impact. Doumbia-Henry said water transportation workers will need to learn new skills to be ready for future job opportunities. "New and advancing technologies have already transformed maritime transportation and will continue to do so at all levels," she said. "[This includes how] ships are designed, constructed, equipped and operated, and will certainly significantly impact personnel, both onboard and onshore, including the new skill sets that will be required."

Mates or deck officers fill in for the captain when he or she is away. Large ships have a first, second, and third mate. These workers divide the duties for operating the ship. These include taking care of cargo or passengers, navigating the watercraft, and ensuring the ship's safety.

Ship pilots direct their water vessels through smaller waterways, such as river harbors. A watercraft's sailors, or

WATER TRANSPORTATION WORKERS

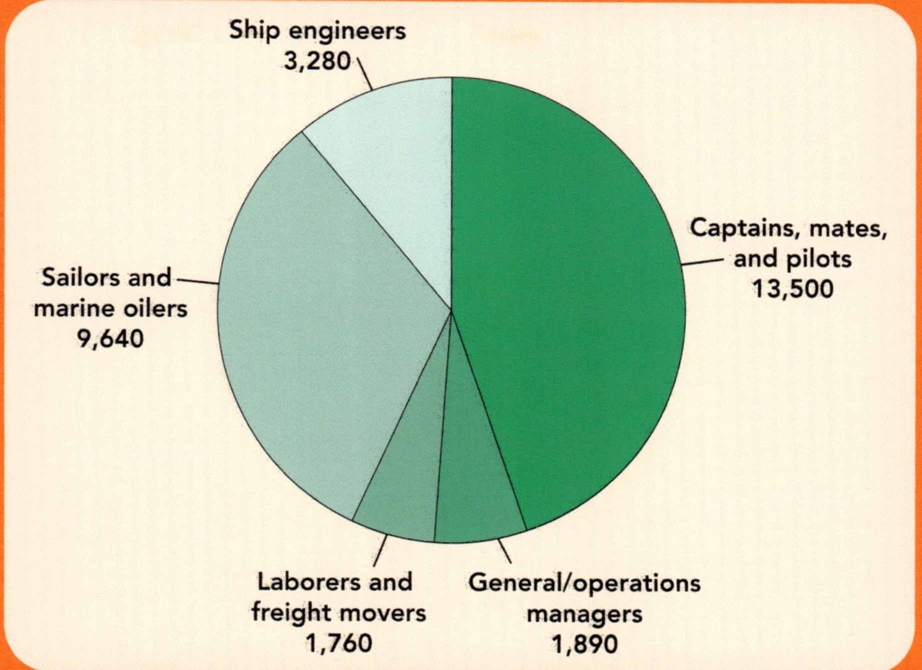

In 2021, many US water transportation workers were captains, mates, and pilots. How does that compare to what is described in the chapter? Why do you think more people choose these jobs?

deckhands, operate and maintain the ship's equipment. Pieces of special equipment, such as a ship's engine and generator, are cared for by ship engineers. Marine oilers work with these engineers, helping to keep machinery in good working condition.

EDUCATION AND TRAINING

All people who work on ships that fly the US flag must get a special certificate from the US Transportation Security Administration (TSA). Except for new entry-level sailors and marine oilers, most other water transportation workers complete training programs approved by the US Coast Guard. Some people who complete these programs choose to work in the military. Often, people with college degrees from qualifying marine schools are preferred for military jobs.

During training, water transportation workers develop important skills to use on the job. They must learn how to steer and operate controls on a watercraft. They must also practice being aware of their surroundings while out on the water. It's helpful for water transportation workers to be strong and work well with their hands. They often need to handle heavy equipment.

STRAIGHT TO THE SOURCE

Camille Simbulan works for the Associated Marine Officer's and Seamen's Union in the Philippines. She believes steps need to be taken to attract more young people to jobs in water transportation:

> *The maritime industry must start actively engaging with and investing in the next generation of seafarers if it wants to keep supply chains intact over the next decades. Young people today are very dynamic, empowered and are genuinely passionate about using their talents to create a positive impact. They will go where they feel valued, respected, and inspired, so the maritime industry needs to step up.*

Source: "Young Maritime Professionals Identify Six Areas for Improvement to Make the Maritime Industry More Attractive," *Global Maritime Forum*, 22 Sept. 2022, globalmaritimeforum.org. Accessed 25 Sept. 2022.

BACK IT UP

The author of this passage is using evidence to support a point. Write a paragraph describing the point the author is making. Then write down two or three pieces of evidence the author uses to make the point.

CHAPTER FIVE

TECHNOLOGY AND TRANSPORTATION

New technologies are changing the future of jobs in transportation. Equipment has helped improve vehicle safety and traffic efficiency. Sensors, cameras, and radar continue to be developed. These technologies help transportation workers who work with ground vehicles, trains, aircraft, and water vessels. They provide new ways for vehicles, travelers, and traffic managers to communicate with each other.

Transportation workers use drones to inspect roads and bridges. The drones collect data that helps workers see what needs repairs.

People with electric vehicles can charge their vehicles at home or at public charging stations.

Some experts say that the future is headed toward uncrewed aircraft systems, supersonic aircraft, and passenger trips into outer space. New technologies are also changing how watercraft are built and operated. Some of these technologies involve robotics. Others involve building vehicles from environmentally friendly materials and using cleaner fuel sources.

TRANSPORTATION AND THE ENVIRONMENT

Technologies such as electric vehicles aim to reduce vehicles' impact on the environment. Some people believe that electricity could replace gasoline and diesel fuel as the main way to power vehicles. People are moving away from gasoline and diesel because these fuels release greenhouse gases into the air when they are burned. These gases trap heat in the atmosphere, making the planet hotter. But in 2022, the United States had very few electric vehicles. Only about 1 percent of the country's 250 million cars, SUVs, and smaller trucks were electric.

To increase the number of electric vehicles on the road,

STEPPING UP WITH SENSORS

Sensor technology is now being used to monitor vehicle operations and assist drivers. Some sensors alert transportation workers about accidents and traffic delays. Others sense vehicles in drivers' blind spots, notify drivers about road closures, and even help people plan the fastest routes. Sensors can also help drivers get assistance if they have an emergency. This new technology helps transportation workers do their jobs more safely and efficiently.

new ways of building and maintaining vehicles are needed. Many people who build and maintain vehicles will need to learn different skills to do their jobs. Some people are concerned that transportation workers who don't learn these new skills will need to find other jobs.

THE FUTURE OF VEHICLES

Future vehicles will connect to each other and to the wider transportation system. For instance, a vehicle could alert its driver to watch out for a traffic accident ahead. These technologies can help make driving safer for truck and bus drivers.

In the future, cars with computers and sensors may be able to drive themselves. These autonomous vehicles will adjust their driving based on road conditions and other vehicles. Their human passengers can relax on the way to their destinations. Some transportation drivers may take on new roles as autonomous vehicle operators. They will need to monitor and manage the systems the vehicles use.

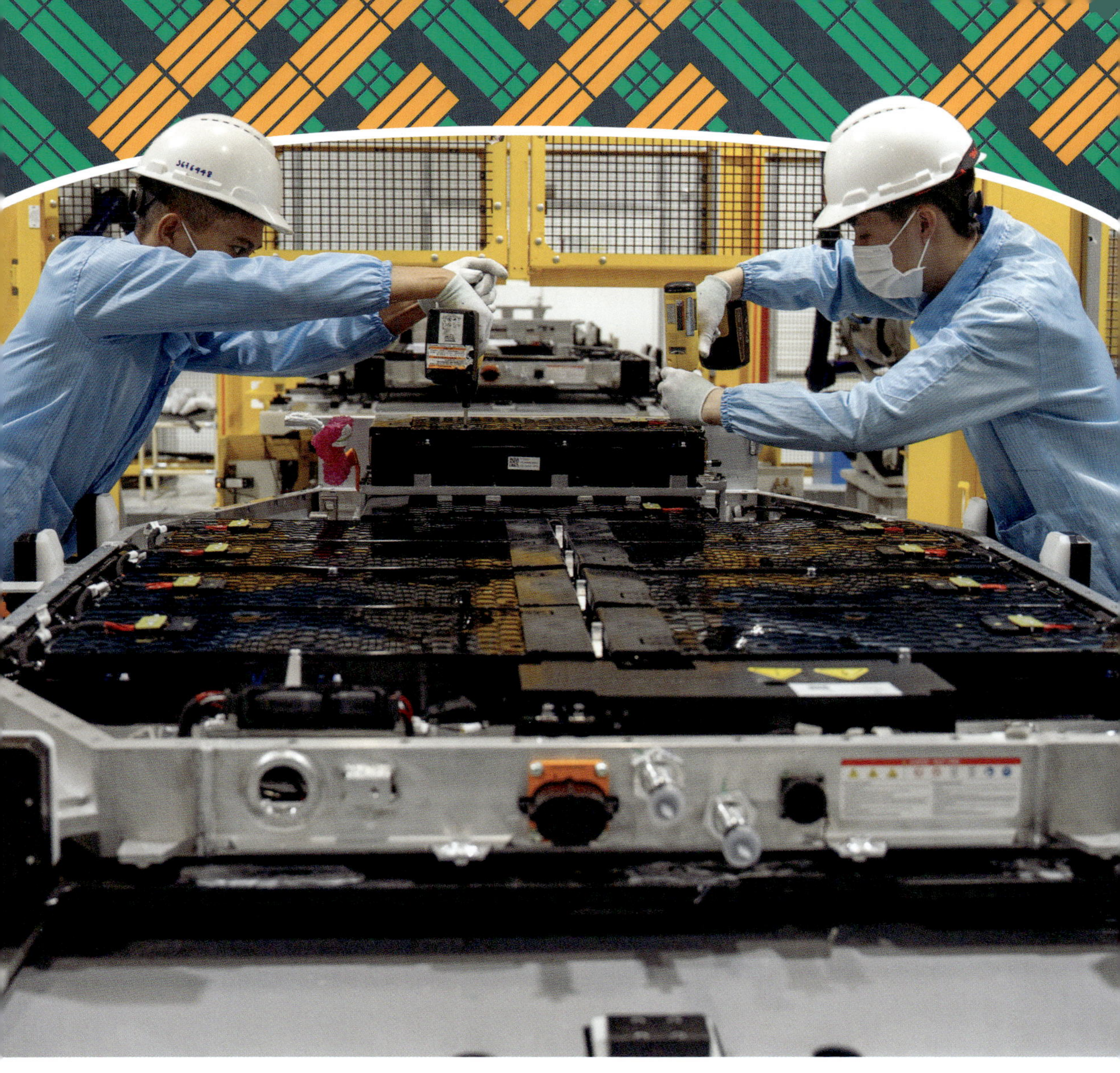

Electric vehicles require large, complex batteries. Workers are needed to design, develop, and build these batteries.

NEW TECHNOLOGY

New electronic systems such as phones and radios help transportation workers do their jobs. Some of these people are traffic management systems integrators. They integrate, or combine, one system with another. These systems include electronic equipment, such as communications technologies and electronic signs. They also include closed-circuit televisions. Systems integrators provide drivers, passengers, and controllers with helpful information. For example, they may program an electronic highway sign to say "accident ahead" after hearing from another source that there's an accident on the roadway.

Transportation workers make it possible for people to travel where they need to go. Whether on the ground, in the air, or over water, jobs in transportation provide a wide range of ways to transport people and goods efficiently. Transportation workers may even develop new technologies to make transportation faster and safer. No matter the job, working in transportation offers many exciting opportunities.

STRAIGHT TO THE SOURCE

The US Department of Transportation discusses how connected vehicles could change the transportation industry:

> *Connected vehicle safety applications will enable drivers to have 360-degree awareness of hazards and situations they cannot even see. Through in-car warnings, drivers will be alerted to imminent crash situations, such as merging trucks, cars in the driver's blind side, or when a vehicle ahead brakes suddenly. By communicating with roadside infrastructure, drivers will be alerted when they are entering a school zone, if workers are on the roadside, and if an upcoming traffic light is about to change.*

Source: "How Will Connected Vehicles Be Used?" *Intelligent Transportation Systems Joint Program Office*, n.d., its.dot.gov. Accessed 3 Oct. 2022.

WHAT'S THE BIG IDEA?

Take a close look at this passage. What is the main connection being made between the transportation industry and connected vehicles? How will these electronic systems affect the way people and goods are transported? How will they affect how transportation workers communicate?

JOB LIST

Delivery truck drivers pick up, transport, and drop off packages and shipments within a local region.

Tractor-trailer truck drivers transport goods from one place to another. They sometimes transport things across states and across the country.

Airline and commercial pilots fly and navigate airplanes, helicopters, and other aircraft.

Air traffic controllers coordinate the movement of aircraft to maintain safe distances between them.

Locomotive engineers drive trains between stations. They use a variety of controls and monitor operational and safety systems.

Bus drivers and passenger vehicle drivers operate buses, taxis, and other vehicles to transport people from place to place.

Ship captains steer and operate water vessels. They direct a watercraft's crew and coordinate how their boat moves through the water.

Supervisors oversee transportation employees. Their duties include operations of road and equipment repair, traffic, engineering applications, and contracts.

Traffic management systems integrators set up and install devices used in traffic management, such as closed-circuit TV, vehicle detection, and electronic signs.

Flight attendants provide routine services and respond to emergencies to ensure the safety and comfort of airline passengers.

STOP AND THINK

Tell the Tale

Chapter One of this book discusses a rail traffic controller's experience responding to an obstacle on a railroad track. Imagine you are a rail traffic controller in a similar situation. Write 200 words about who you would contact and what you would do. How would you keep everyone safe and get the train moving again?

Say What?

Learning about different jobs in transportation can mean learning a lot of new vocabulary. Find five words in this book you've never heard before. Use a dictionary to find out what they mean. Then write the meanings in your own words and use each word in a new sentence.

Take a Stand

New technologies in transportation could replace jobs that people currently have. This could cause established workers to lose their jobs or take on new tasks in order to stay employed. Do you think this is a good or bad thing? Why?

You Are There

This book discusses how new technology could change the future of transportation. Imagine you are in a city where all the cars are self-driving. Write a letter home telling your friends what it's like. How do self-driving cars help people in the city? How do the cars keep people safe? Are there any dangers to having self-driving cars? Be sure to add plenty of detail to your notes.

GLOSSARY

autonomous vehicle
a vehicle that can operate without a human driver

aviator
the operator or pilot of an aircraft

cargo
goods or products carried in a vehicle

freight
products, goods, or merchandise transported in a vehicle

locomotive
a railway vehicle that provides the moving power for a train

passenger vehicle
a motor vehicle designed to carry passengers on highways and streets

radar
an electronic system that uses radio waves to detect objects

route
a road or pathway used to travel from one place to another

sensor
an electronic device that detects and responds to something from the environment

ONLINE RESOURCES

To learn more about jobs in transportation, visit our free resource websites below.

Visit **abdocorelibrary.com** or scan this QR code for free Common Core resources for teachers and students, including vetted activities, multimedia, and booklinks, for deeper subject comprehension.

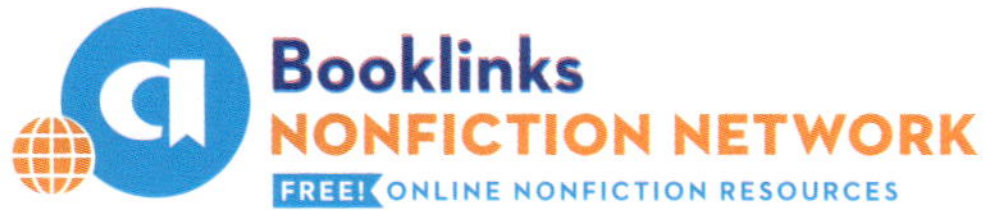

Visit **abdobooklinks.com** or scan this QR code for free additional online weblinks for further learning. These links are routinely monitored and updated to provide the most current information available.

LEARN MORE

Dickmann, Nancy. *The Impact of Travel and Transportation.* Crabtree, 2020.

Eschbach, Christina. *Inside Electric Cars.* Abdo, 2019.

INDEX

About the Author

Karen Maserjian Shan has written for newspapers, magazines, and online publications. She cofounded Children's Writers of the Hudson Valley and is a past committee member for the New York: Eastern Upstate Chapter of the Society of Children's Book Writers and Illustrators.